15 Minutes !!

Author
Re-Gina Barnes
Version Mommy, Daddy

Illustrations inspired by
Dakota Jay Brooks

Illustrator
Alexandra Rotariu

Author: Re-Gina Barnes and 15 Minutes

THIS SING-ALONG BOOK PAIRED WITH THE 15 MINUTES SONG IS DESIGNED IN AN INNOVATIVE WAY TO INTRODUCE THE IMPORTANCE OF HOW 15 MINUTES A DAY OF READING WILL HELP MOTIVATE PARENTS AND GUARDIANS IN THE DEVELOPMENT OF THEIR LOVE ONES.

THIS ROUTINE CAN BECOME A MUSICAL LANDSCAPE TO CULTIVATE THOSE MUCH-NEEDED SKILLS SUCH AS GROSS MOTOR, FINE MOTOR, READING READINESS, SCIENTIFIC EXPLORATION, RHYTHMS, RHYMING, AND MATHEMATICAL SKILLS. THIS SING-ALONG CREATES AND DISPLAYS A SOCIAL- EMOTIONAL ATMOSPHERE AS WELL.

I PRAY YOU AND YOUR FAMILY ENJOY THIS SING-ALONG PROJECT AS MUCH AS MY GRANDCHILDREN AND I ENJOYED CREATING IT!

15 Minutes Song Tracks

Copyright 2022 Regina Barnes
First Edition
Version: Mommy, Daddy
All Rights Reserved.
No part of this book may be used or reproduced in any manner whatsoever without written permission.

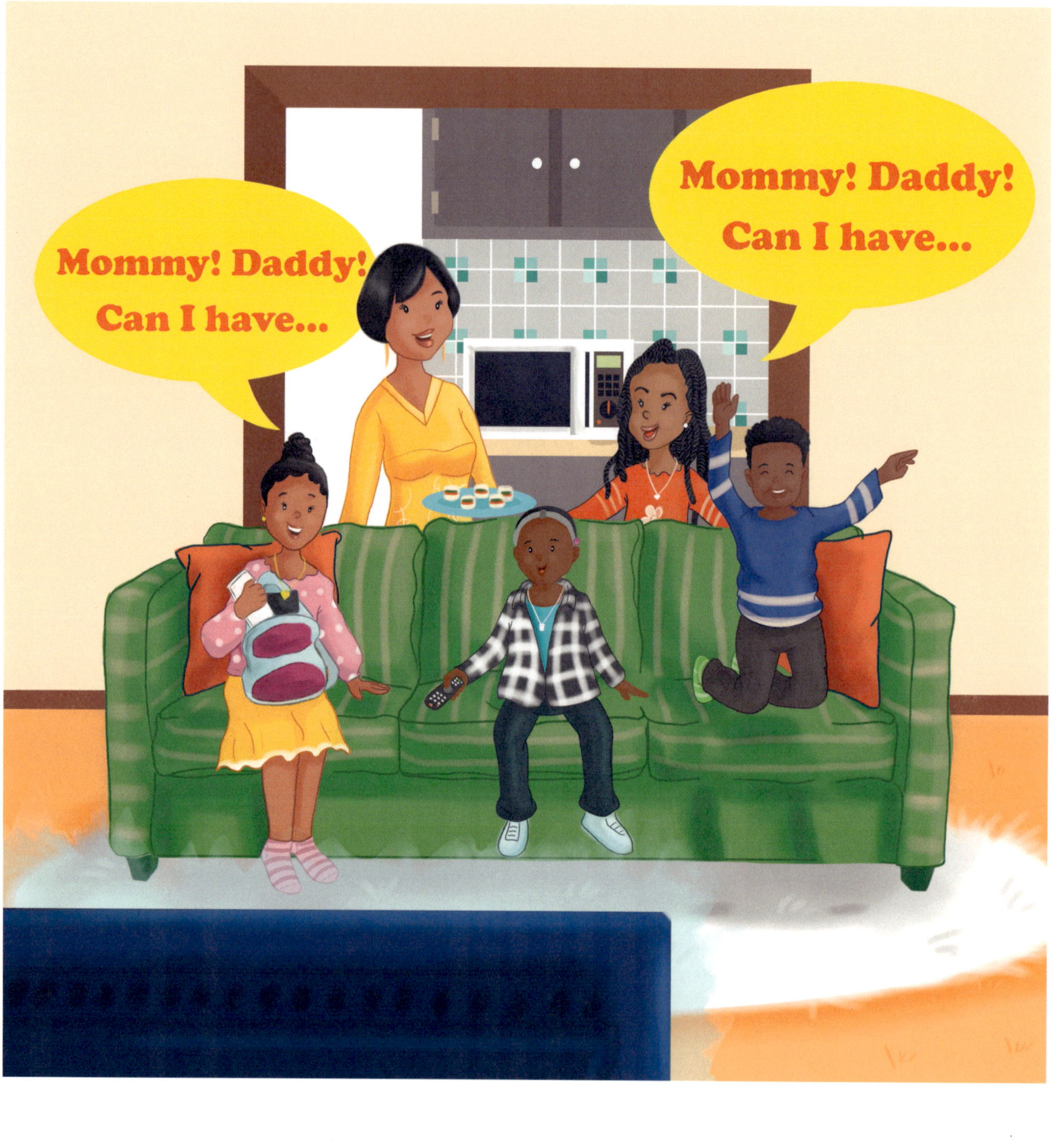
Mommy! Daddy! Can I have...
Mommy! Daddy! Can I have...

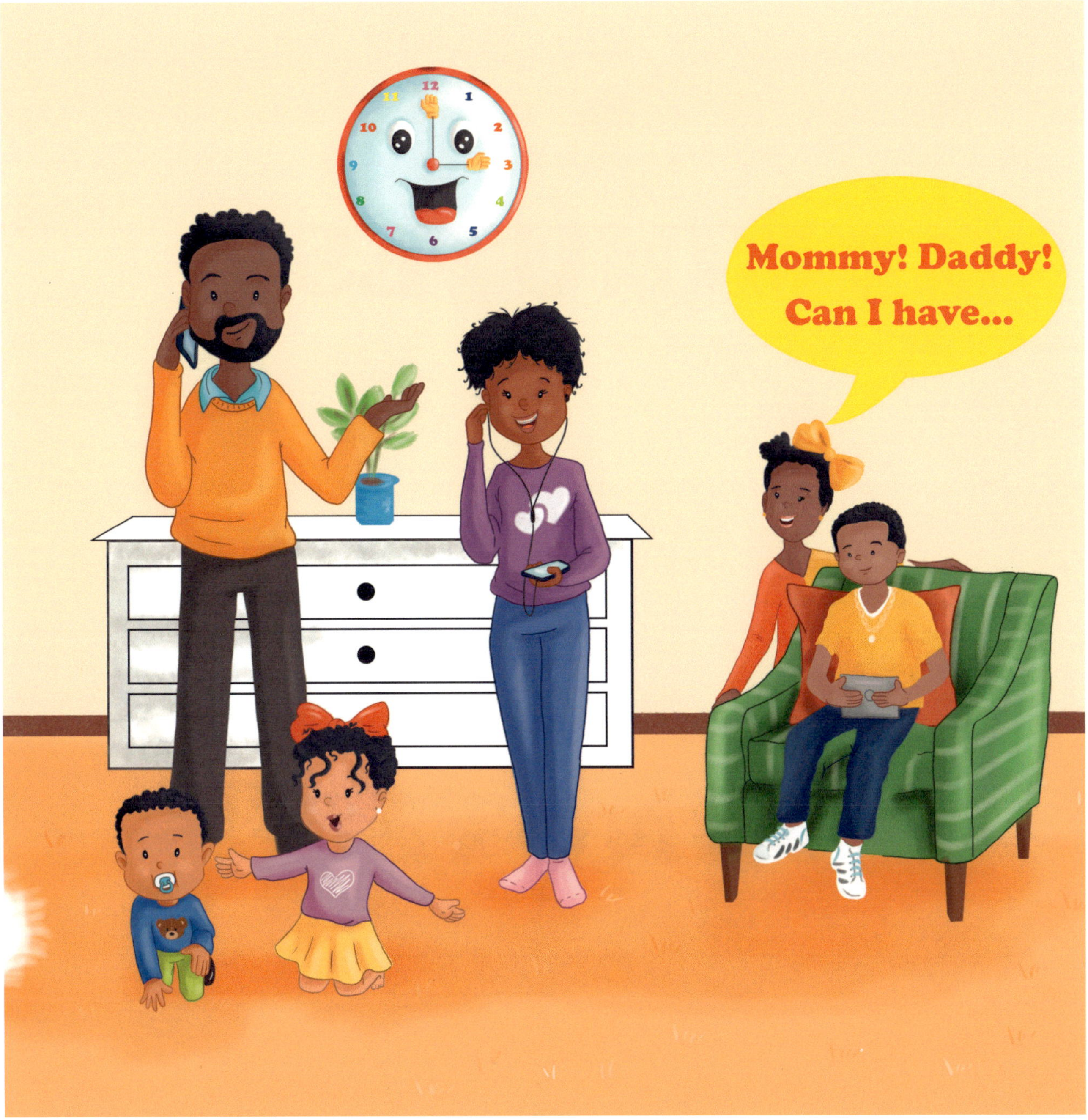
Mommy! Daddy!
Can I have...

15 MINUTES ?

15 MINUTES ?

15 MINUTES ?

TO HELP KEEP THE

BAD GRADES AWAY.

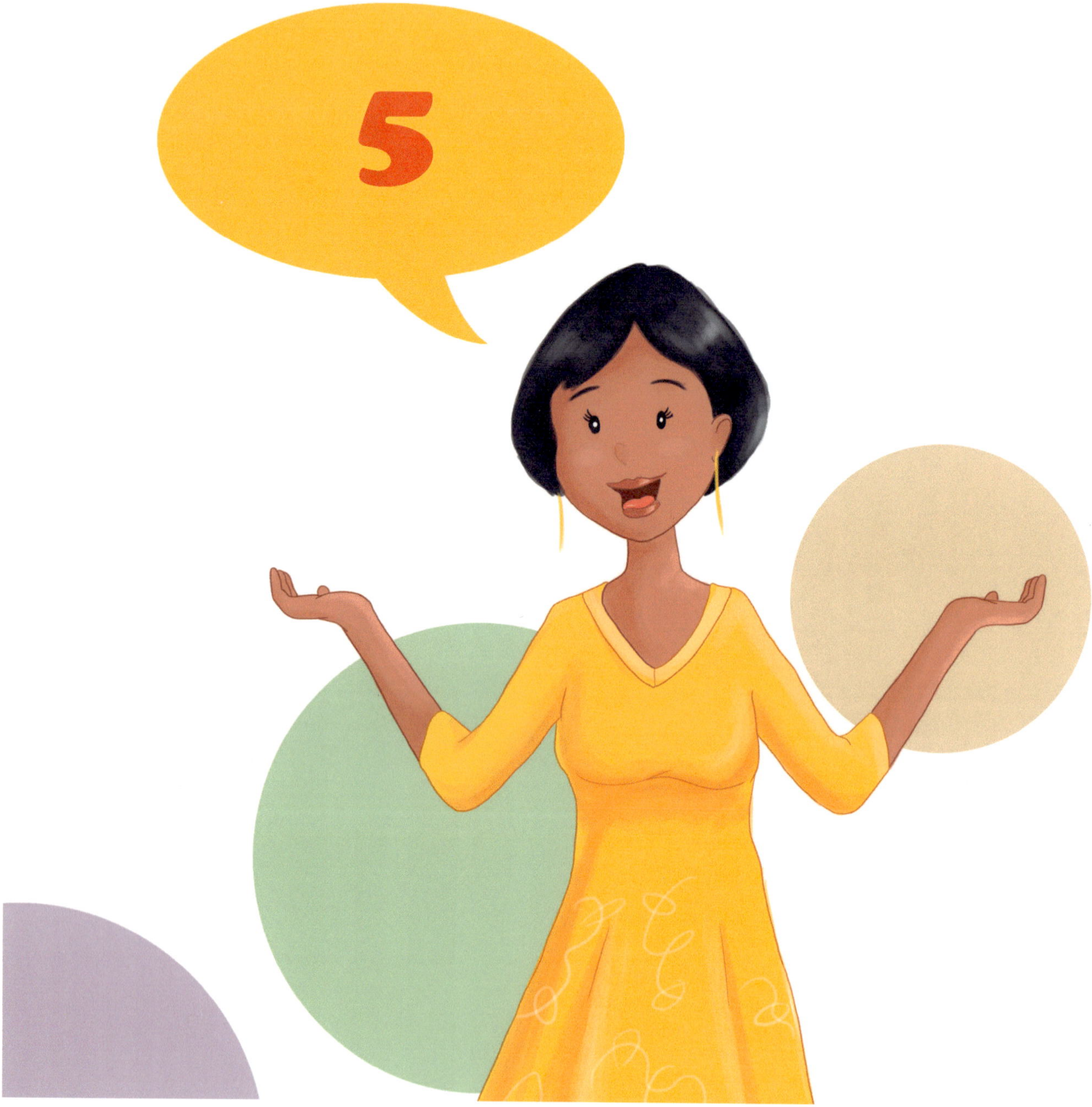
5

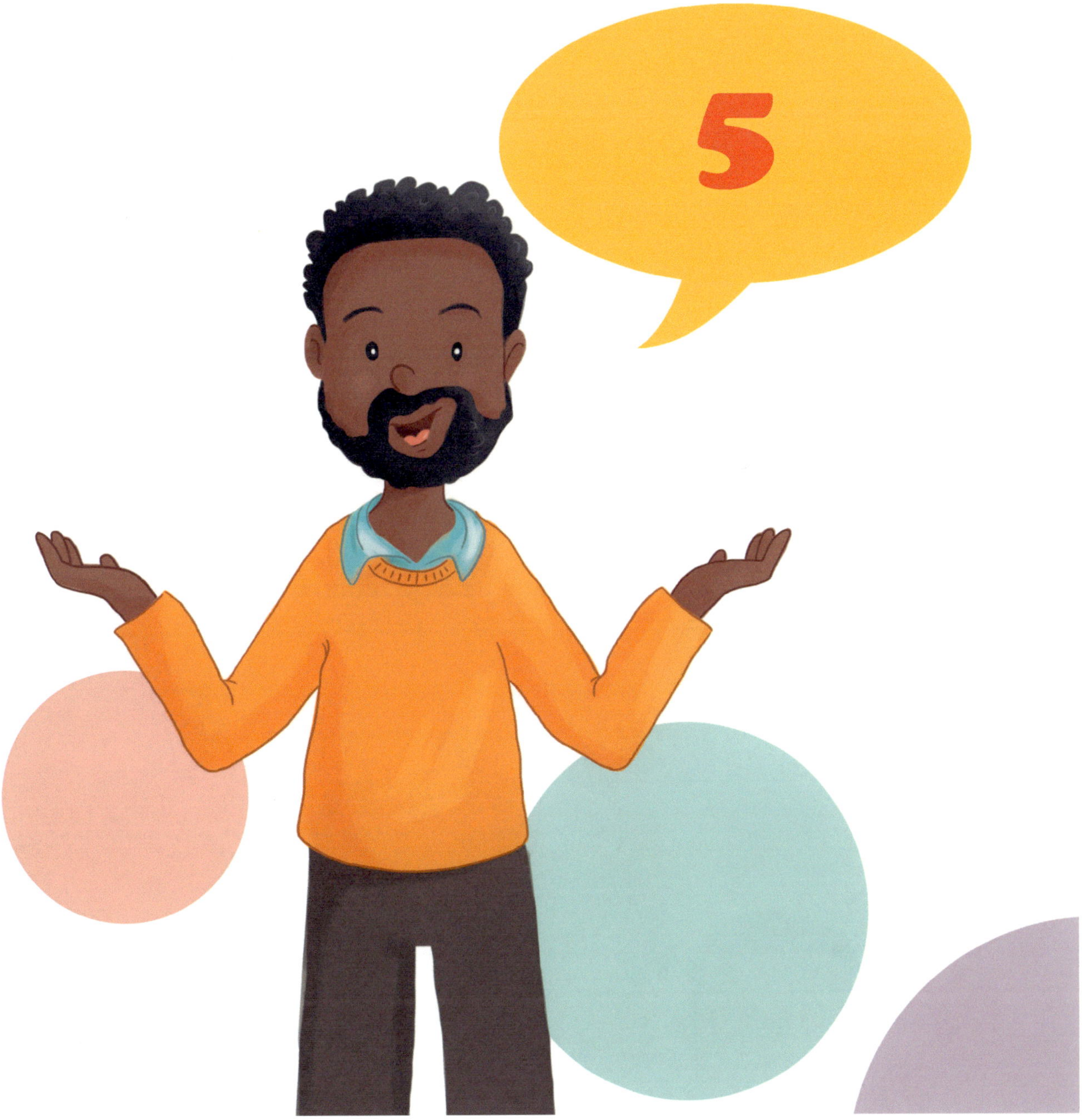
5

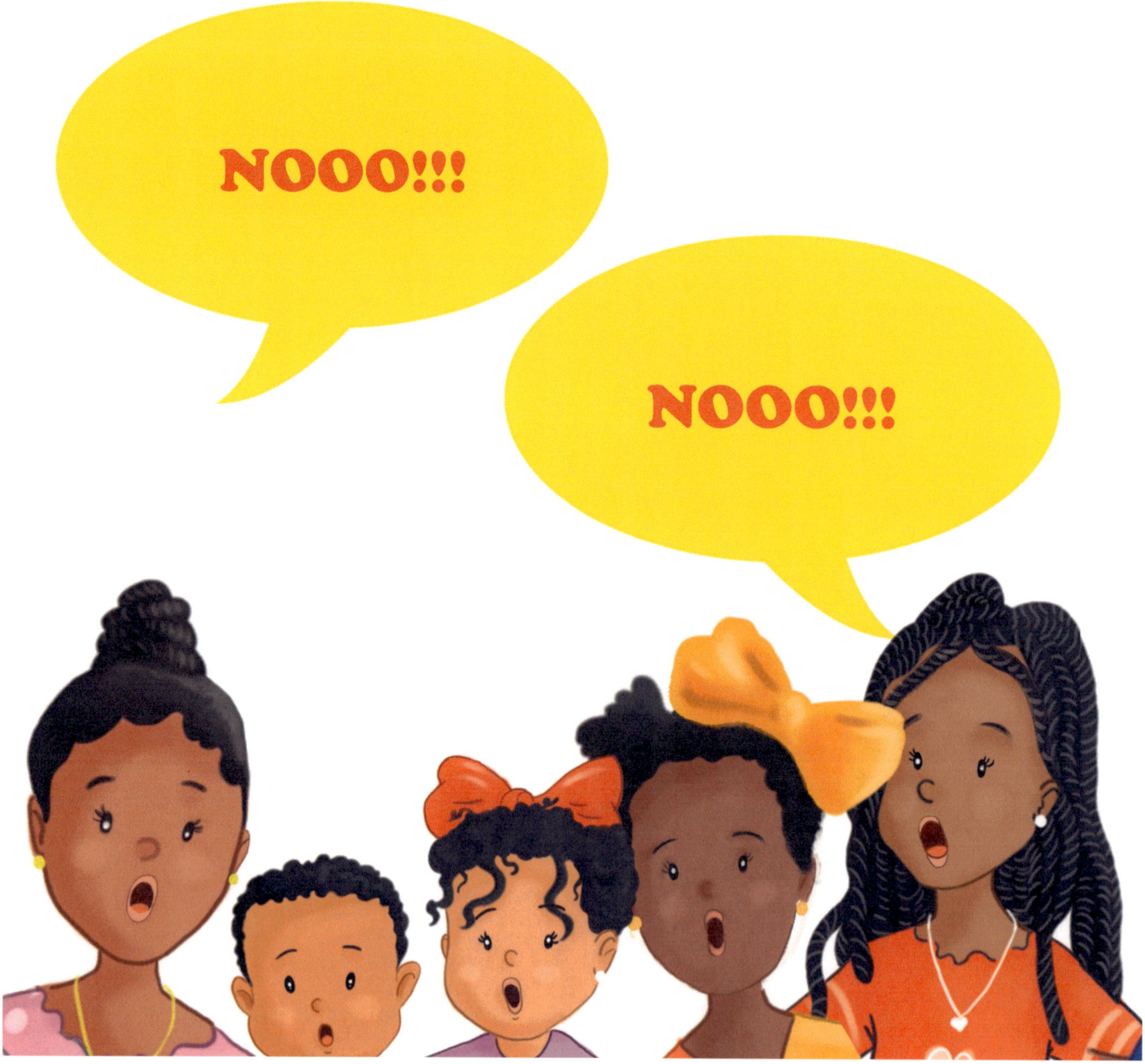
NOOO!!!
NOOO!!!

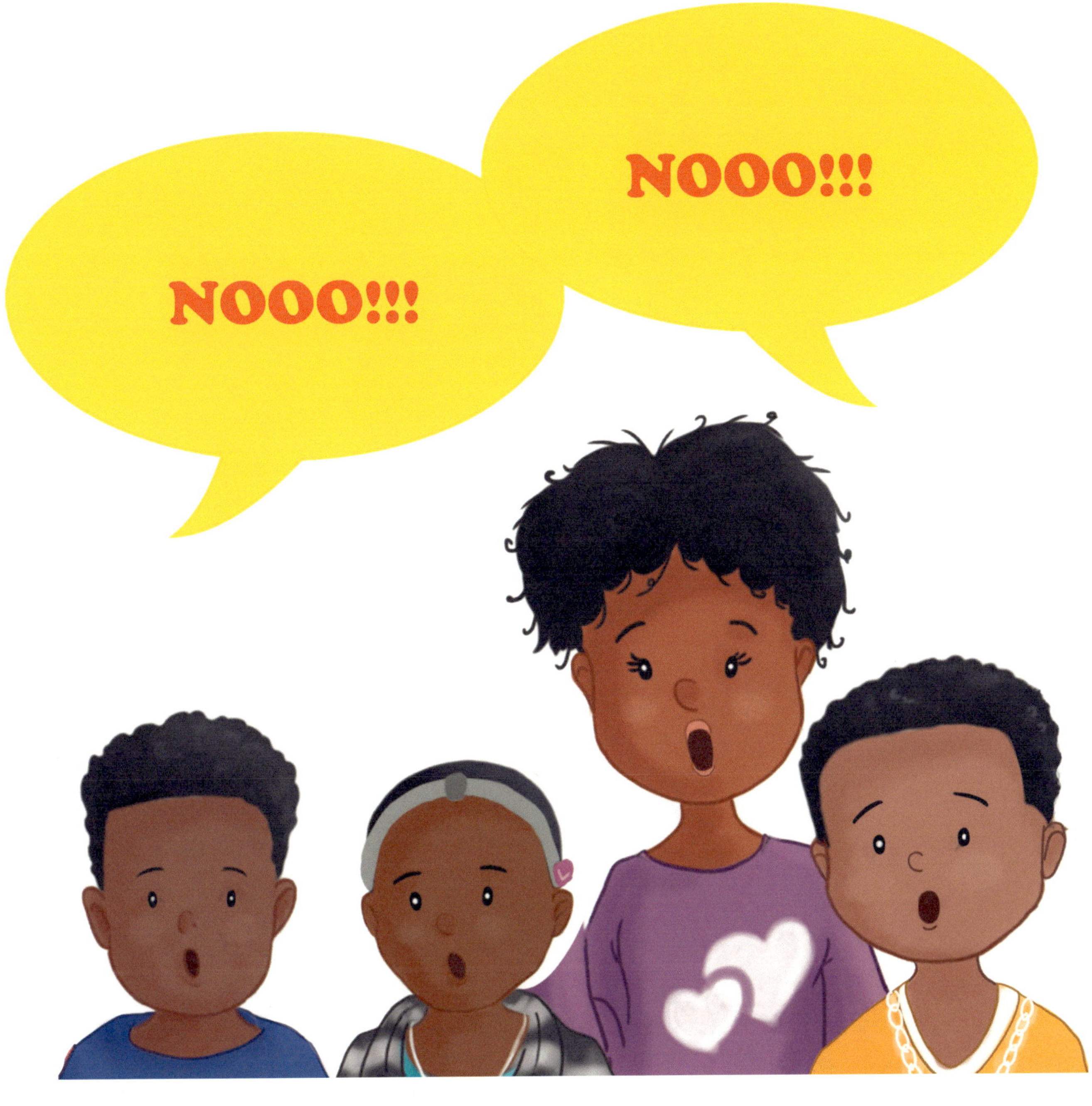
NOOO!!!
NOOO!!!

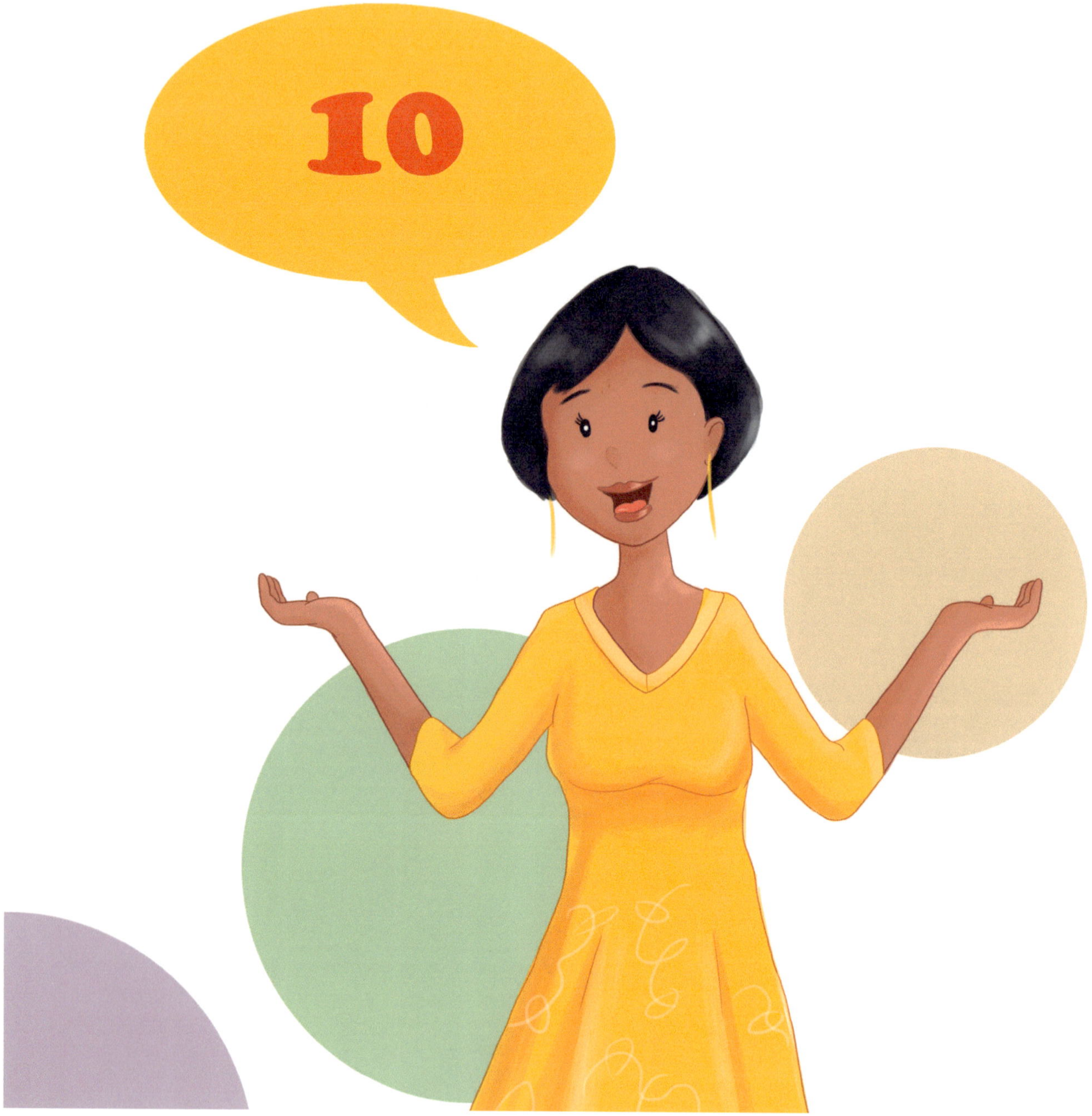
10

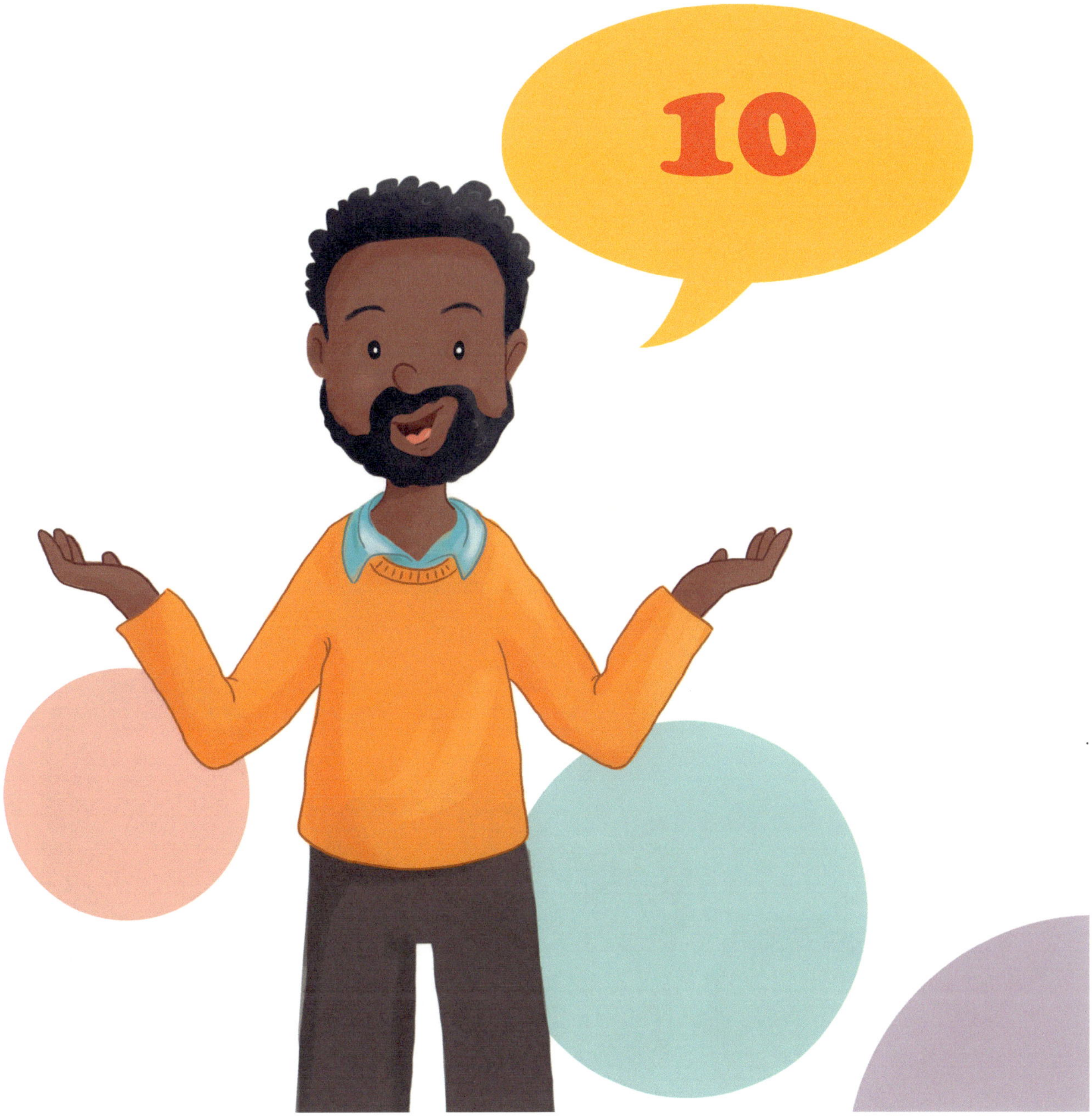
10

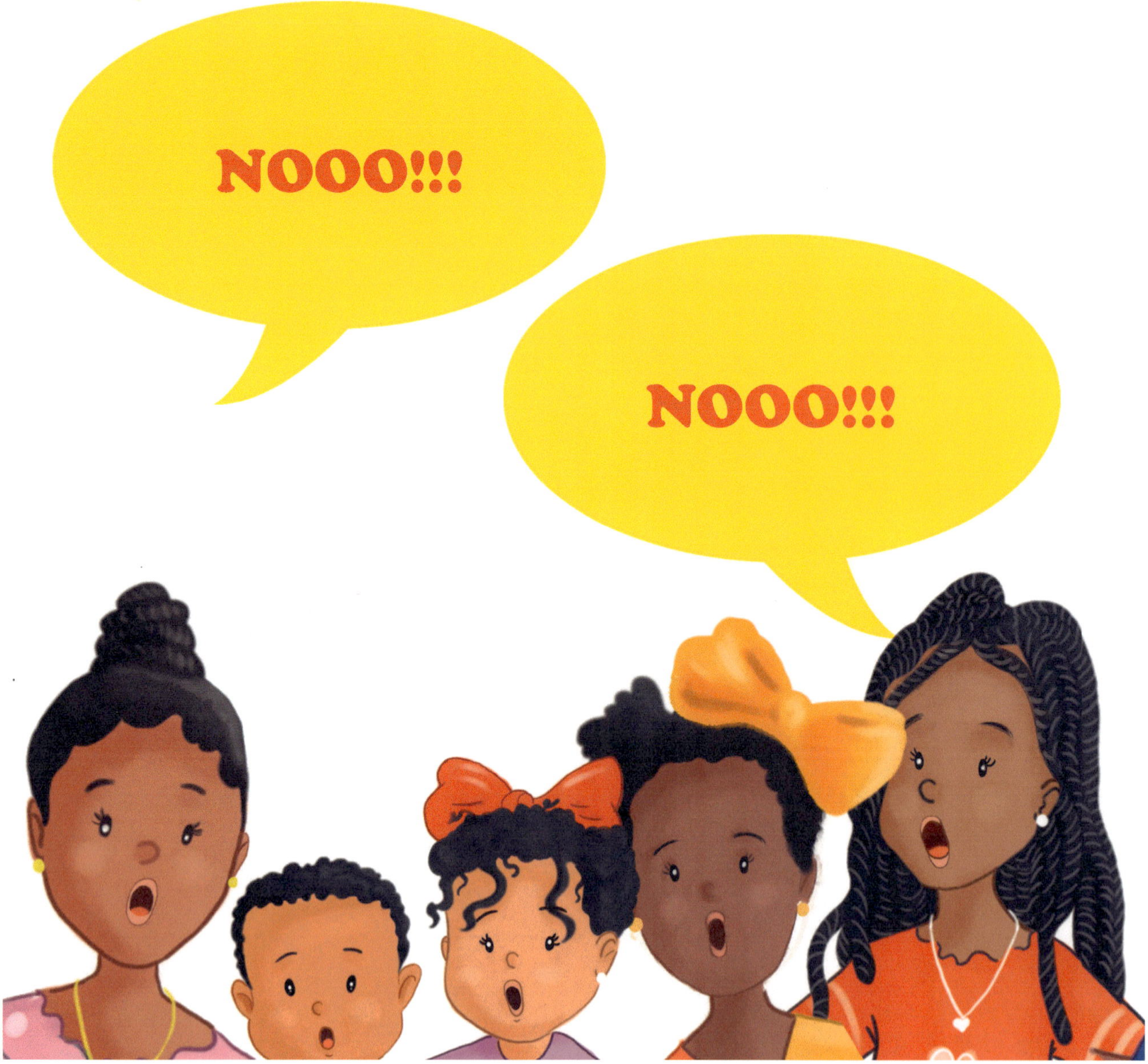
NOOO!!!
NOOO!!!

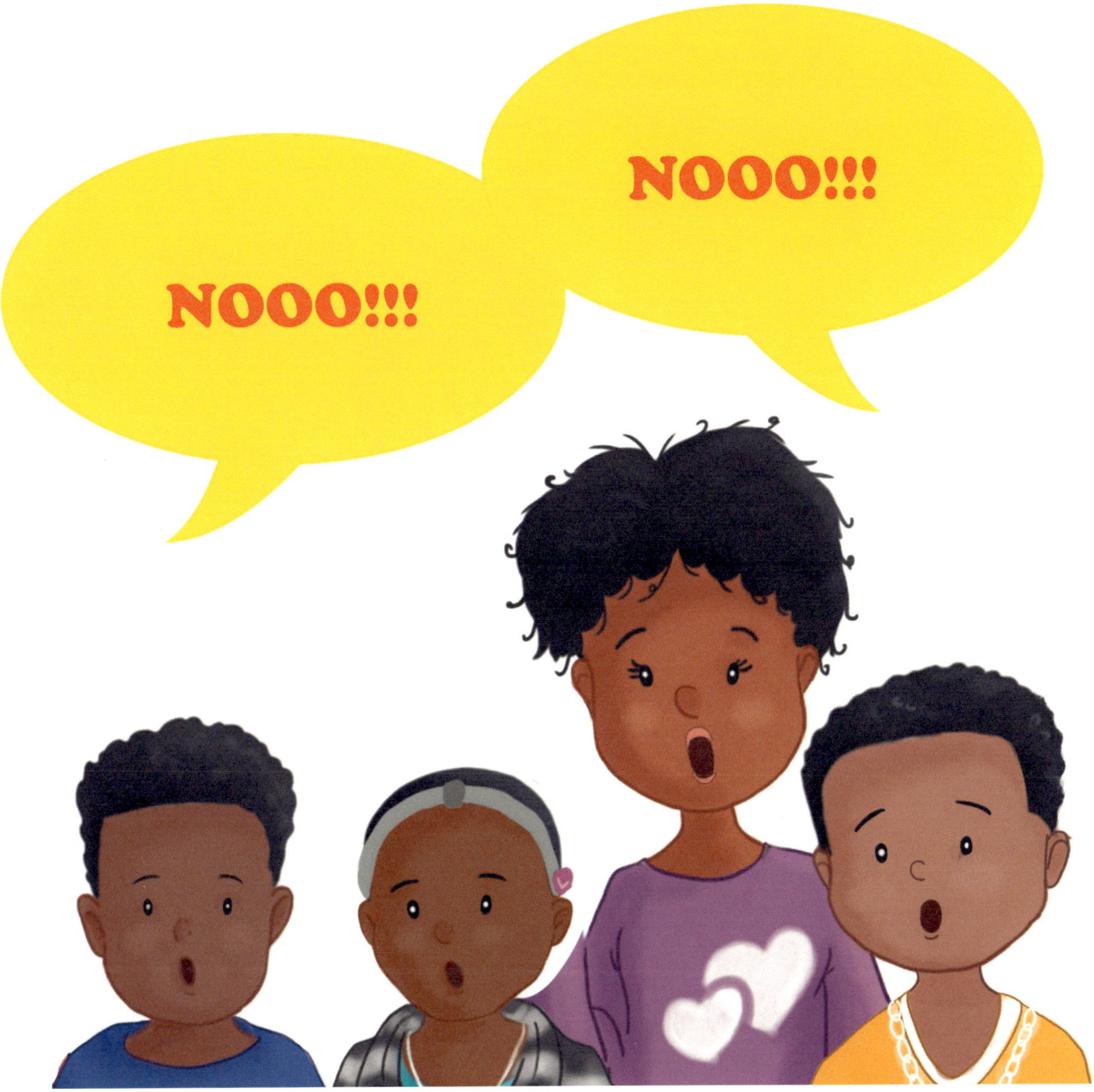
NOOO!!!
NOOO!!!

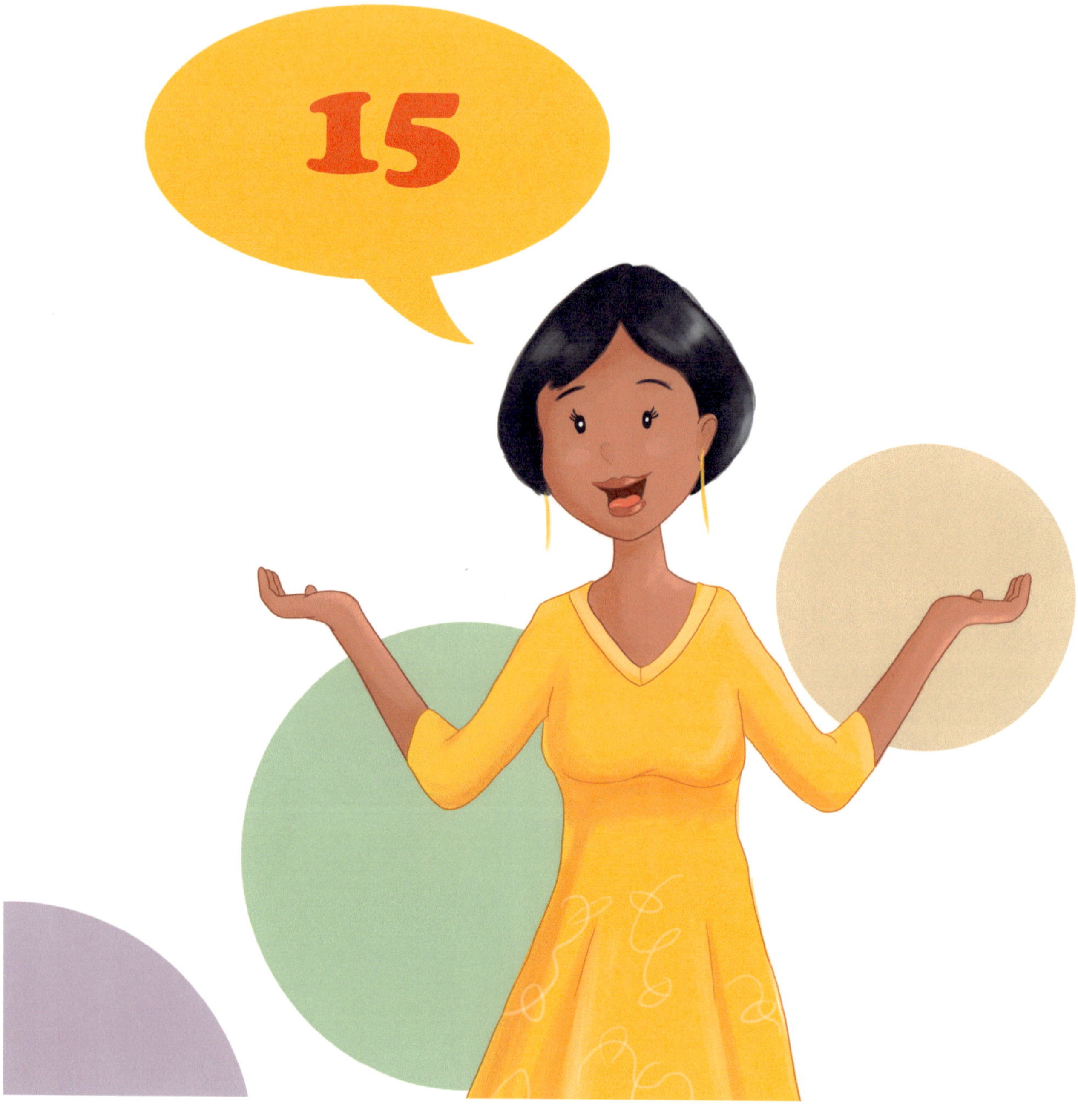
15

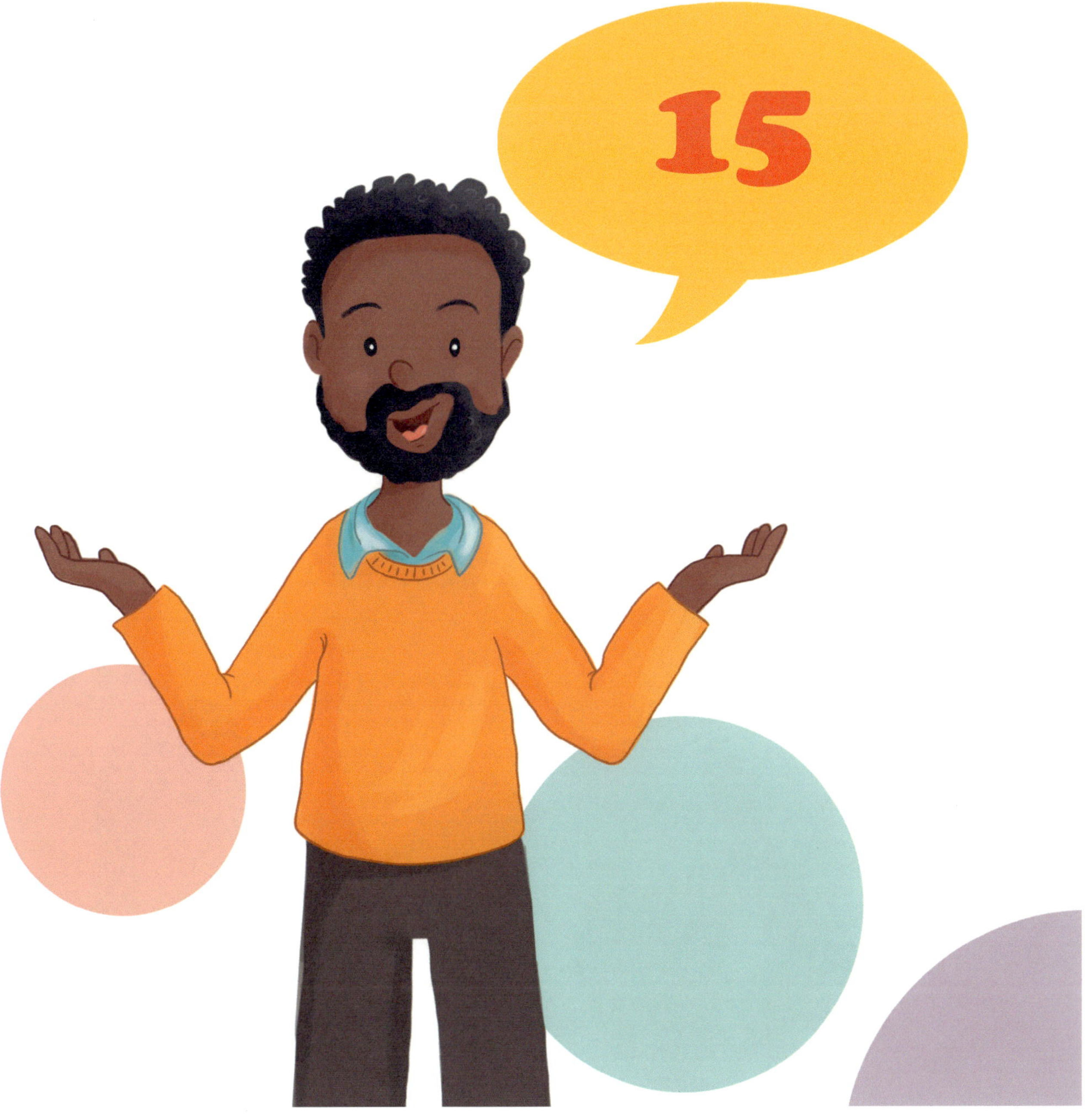
15

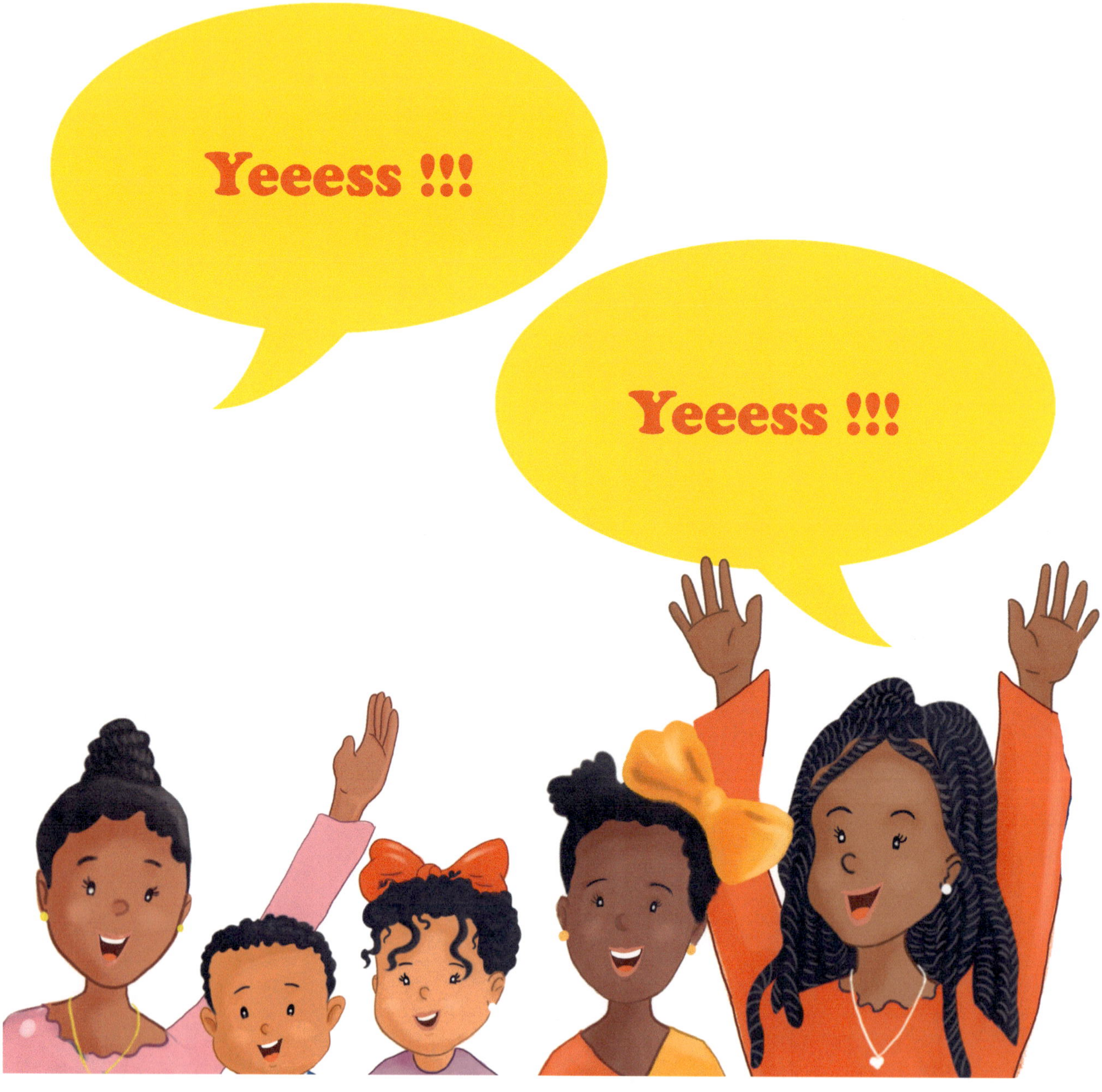
Yeeess !!!
Yeeess !!!

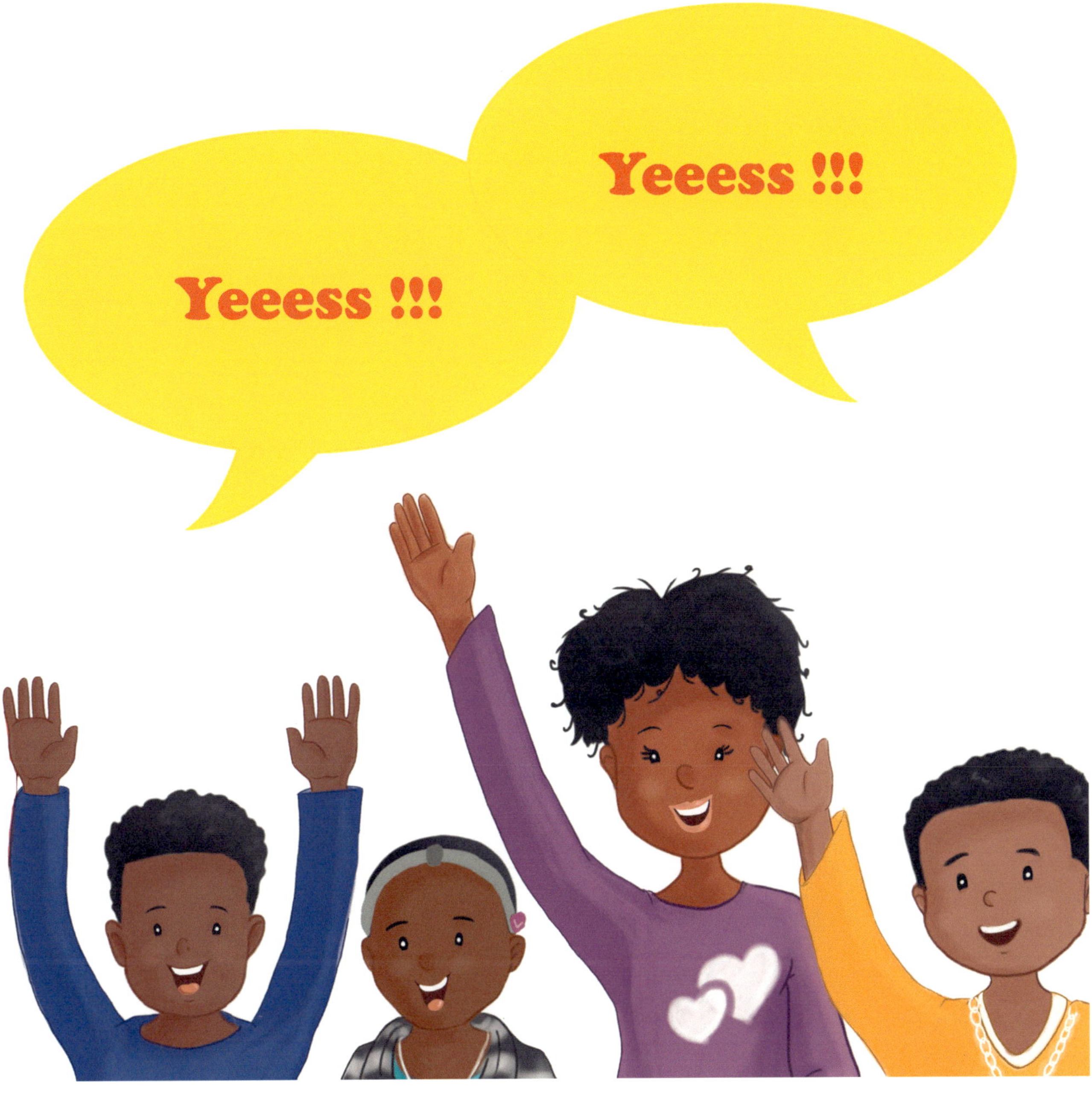
Yeeess !!!
Yeeess !!!

A

DAY

15 MINUTES

15 MINUTES

15 MINUTES

TO HELP KEEP THE

TO HELP KEEP THE

TO HELP KEEP THE

BAD GRADES AWAY.

BAD GRADES AWAY.

BAD GRADES AWAYYYY

Do 15 MINUTES!!

YAH!

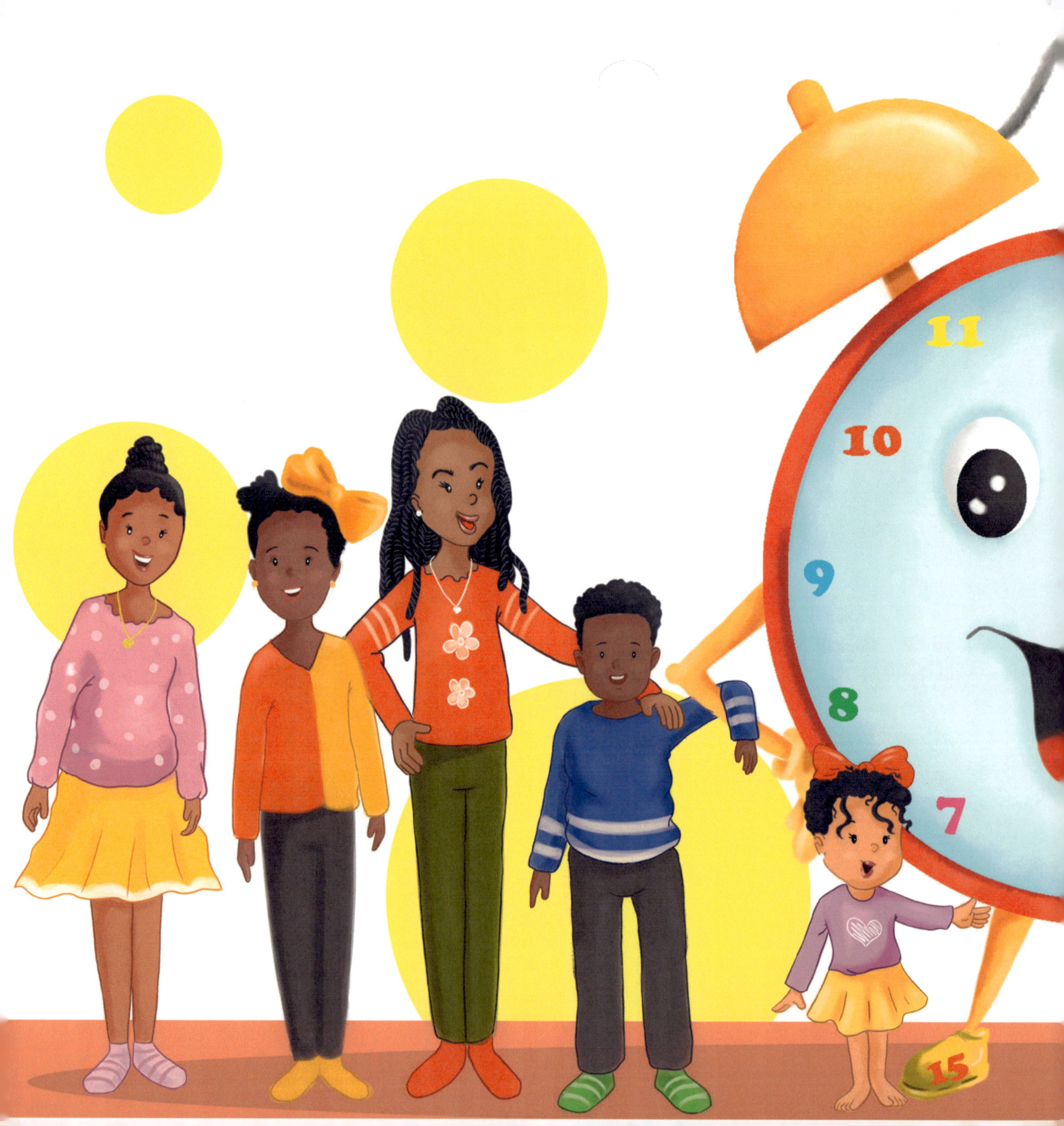
11
10
9
8
7
15

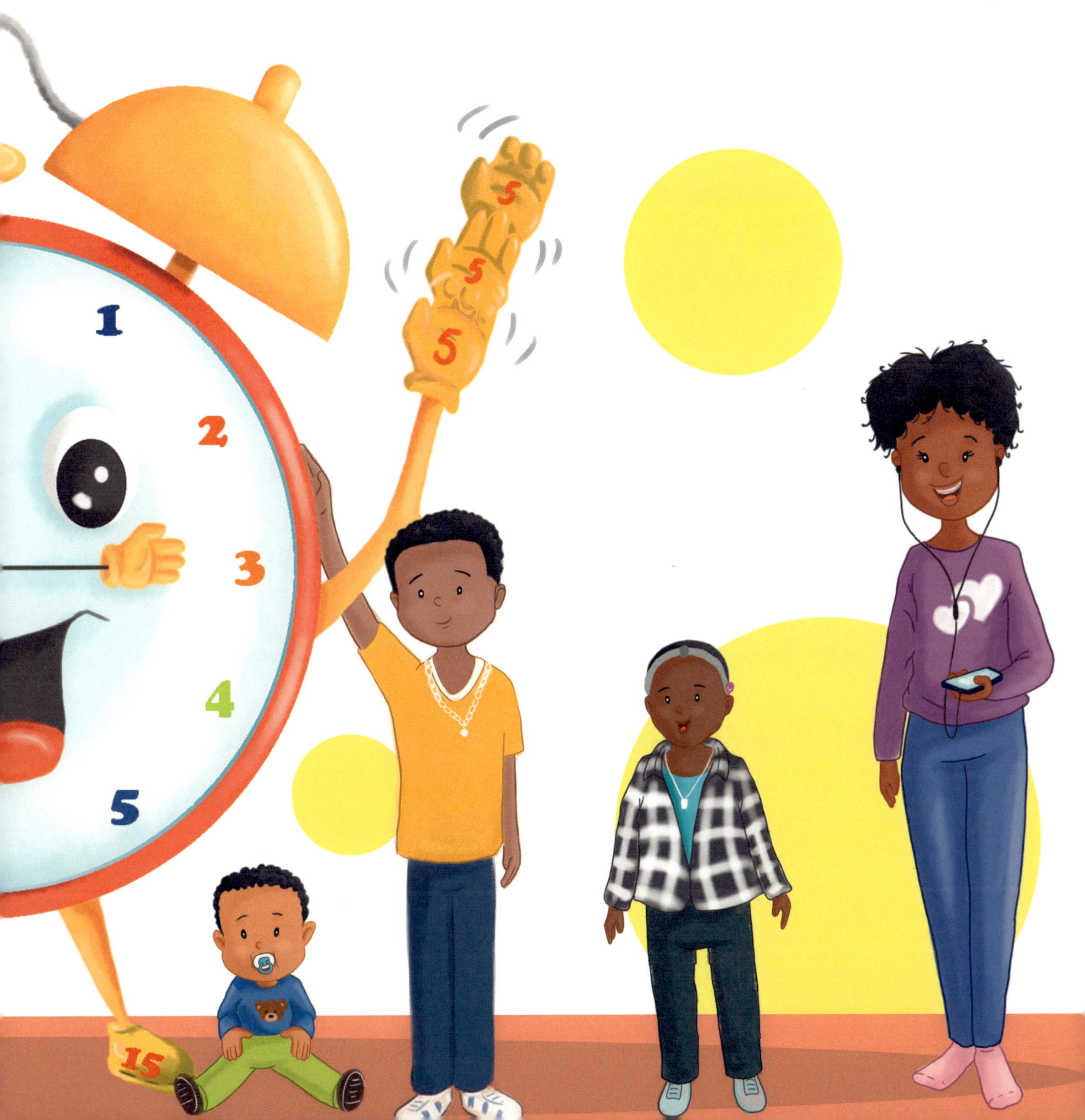
5
5
5
1
2
3
4
5
15

The next pages are instructional pages to communicate how maximizing 15 minutes a day in a variety of environments will help your child/student make good grades and keep the bad grades away.

Good Grades

S

A

B

C

Bad Grades

U

D

F

0 (Zero)

Communication Places

"Home"

Communication Places

"School"

Communication Places

"Traffic"

Communication Places

"Grocery Store"

Communication Places

"Mall"

Communication Places

"Restaurant"

Communication Places

"Church"

Communication Places

"State Fair"

Communication Places

"Park"

Communication Places

"Picnic"

Communication Places

"Sport Events"

Communication Places

"Beach"

Communication Places

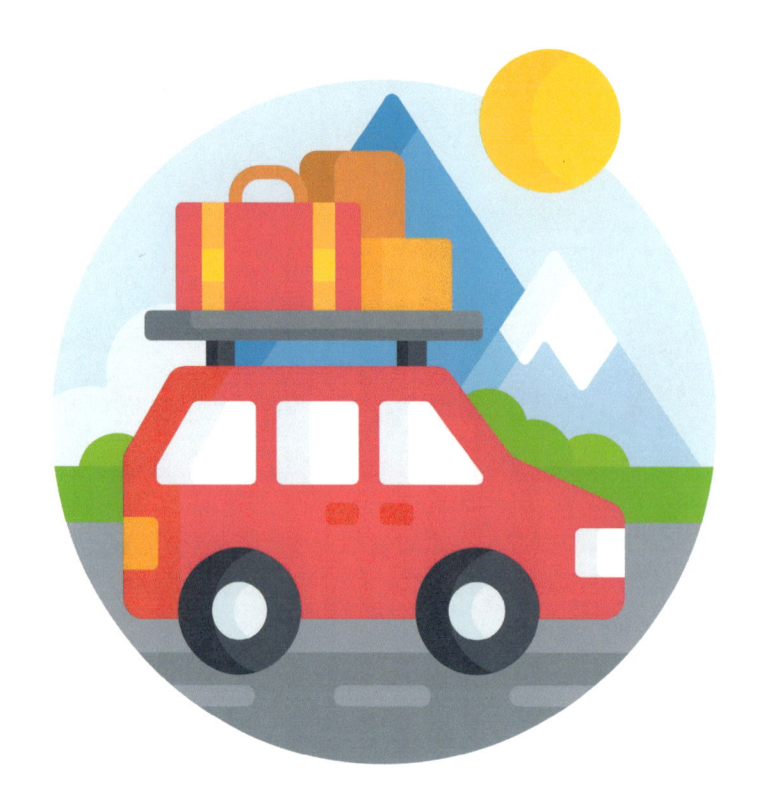

"Family Road Trip"

Communication Places

"Fishing"

Communication Places

"Camping"

Communication Places

"Hiking"

Communication Places

"Hunting"

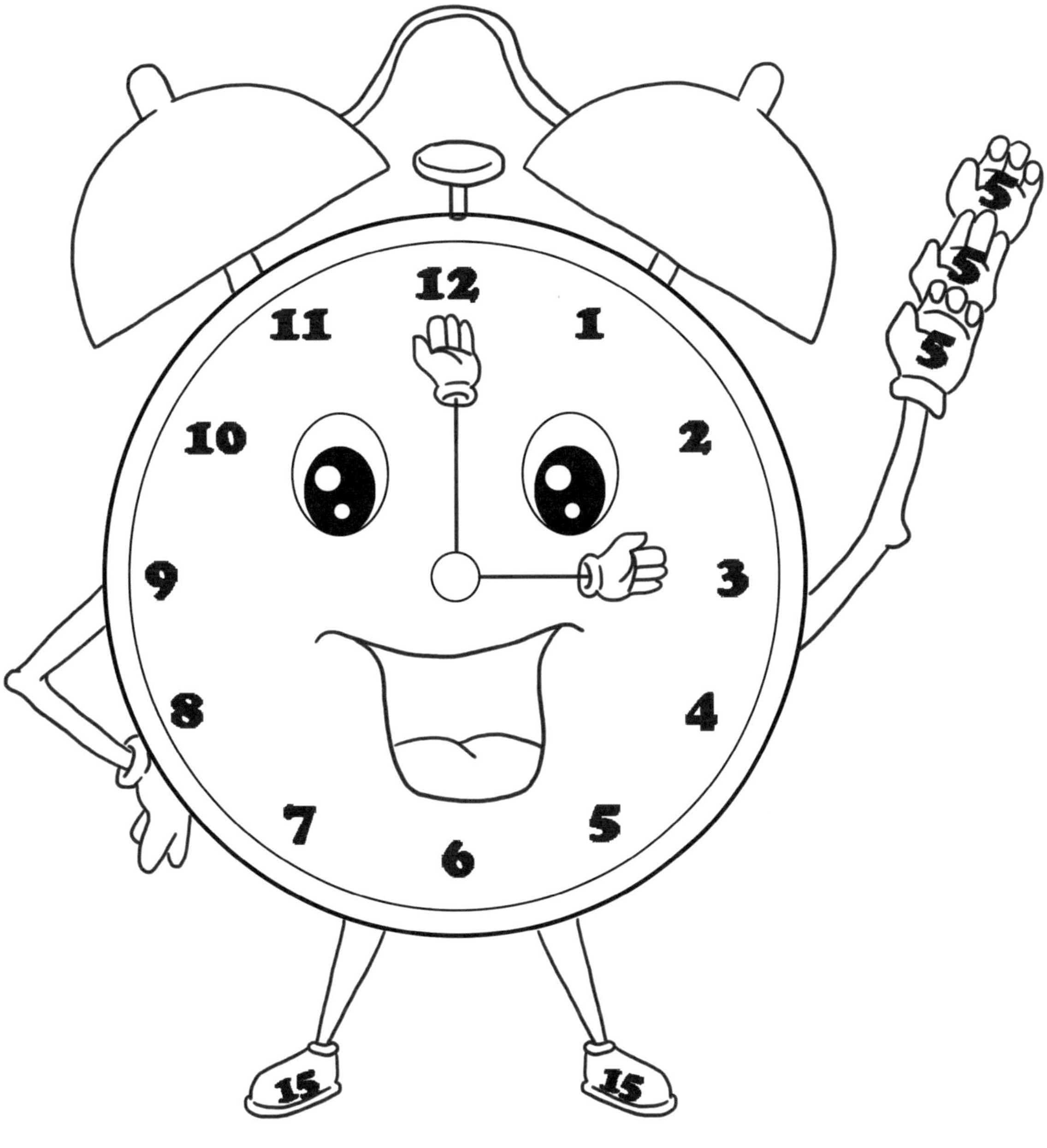
12
1
2
3
4
5
6
7
8
9
10
11
5
5
5
15
15

Made in the USA
Columbia, SC
13 September 2024